P9-DDR-095

CHINESE NEW YEAR

CHINESE NEW YEAR

By Tricia Brown

Photographs by Fran Ortiz

Henry Holt and Company ◆ New York

Published by Henry Holt and Company, Inc.,
521 Fifth Avenue, New York, New York 10175.
Published in Canada by Fitzhenry & Whiteside Limited,
195 Allstate Parkway, Markham, Ontario L3R 4T8.

Library of Congress Cataloging in Publication Data
Brown, Tricia.
Chinese New Year.
Summary: Text and photographs depict the celebration
of Chinese New Year by Chinese Americans living in
San Francisco's Chinatown.
1. New Year—China—Juvenile literature.   2. China—
Social life and customs—Juvenile literature.
3. Chinese Americans—Social life and customs—
Juvenile literature.   [1. New Year—China,
2. China—Social life and customs.   3. Chinese Americans—
Social life and customs] I. Ortiz, Fran, ill. II. Title.
GT4905.B76   1987   394.2'683   87-8532
ISBN: 0-8050-0497-1

First Edition

Designer: Victoria Hartman
Printed in the United States of America
10 9 8 7 6 5 4 3 2 1

ISBN 0-8050-0497-1

Acknowledgments

The author and photographer gratefully acknowledge
the following persons whose cooperation, support, and
enthusiasm made this book possible: Marijane Lee,
Chinese Culture Center; Wylie Wong, Wylie Wong Asian
Art and Antiquities; Emily L. Newell, Oriental Porcelain
Gallery; Corrine Tsang, Chinese bilingual teacher,
Garfield School; Carolyn Nyeh, ESL Bilingual Resource
Teacher, Garfield School; Pastor George Wong, Kong
Chow Temple; Doris Tseng, Chinatown Library; Judy
Yung, Head Librarian, Asian Library, University of
California at Berkeley; Chinese Historical Society of
America; Patrick Andersen, Managing Editor, *Asian
Week*; John Chin, Chun Har Chin, Lawrence Lo, Betty
Lo, Martin Lo, Kimberly Lo, Yuet Sum Mak, Chun Wah
Chin, Justina Cheung, Christina Wang, Cornelia Huang,
Jeffrey Lee, Tau Hing, Roger Lee, Allen Leung, Chui
Tim, Mimi LeHot, Wilson Ung, Kate Baker Hanlin, May
Chin, Ron Lee, Bill Chinn, Geraldine Chinn, Jecina Yee,
Catherine Ortiz, Michael Ortiz, Theodore Brown, Barrett
Brown, Andrea Brown, Marc Cheshire, and Julie Amper.

To our Chinese-American friends

FOREWORD

Chinese New Year is a centuries-old spring festival. It has evolved into the holiday celebrated today with each family interpreting the traditions in its own way. It is a time for the gathering of family and friends. It is a time for special foods, gift giving, and firecrackers. It can include a personal moment to reflect on the events of the past year and to plan ahead for the future, or a public one involving the whole community, with festivities such as the celebrated dragon parade.

However the family chooses to celebrate the event, the holiday is always a joyous occasion and a time for a new beginning.

Gung Hay Fat Choy! Wishing you good fortune and happiness!

All over Chinatown, people greet one another with these happy words.

Gung Hay Fat Choy! It is the time of the Chinese New Year!

This is a celebration of spring, and all of the festival traditions reflect the idea of a new beginning. China is an agricultural country. There, life is closely tied to the cycles of planting and harvesting. The New Year Festival, coming after the autumn harvest and before the start of spring, marks the end of one farming year and the beginning of a new one.

The date for the New Year is determined by the Chinese lunar calendar. In this Chinese calendar, a new moon marks the beginning and a full moon the middle of each month. Chinese New Year's Day is the first day of the first month of the Chinese lunar calendar and falls on different days of the Western calendar in different years. It usually occurs somewhere between the middle of January and the middle of February.

This is the Chinese Lunar Calendar Zodiac Chart. This calendar is based on the cycles of the moon. A different animal represents each year for twelve years; then, the cycle repeats itself. Some Chinese believe people born under the sign of a certain animal will exhibit that animal's characteristics.

The festivities last for weeks. They usually begin around the twentieth day of the twelfth lunar month with preparations for the New Year. Everyone joins in housecleaning, which is symbolic of "sweeping out the old, welcoming in the new." Some families put away their knives and scissors. They don't want to risk "cutting their luck" in the coming year.

When the house is clean, the family begins to decorate. Their best New Year's pictures, called *Nin Wah*, are hung at this time. Scrolls called spring couplets are also put up. Spring couplets are always hung in pairs. They are painted with brushes in black ink on large vertical banners of gold-flecked, red paper. These couplets, short poems written in classical Chinese, are expressions of good wishes for the family in the coming year.

Along with the scroll display, the family places arrangements of New Year fruits. Oranges are most often used because the Chinese word for orange sounds like "wealth." Sometimes tangerines are used. The Chinese word for tangerine sounds like "good fortune." Pomelos, large pear-shaped grapefruit, are also used for displays.

A sign often seen in many homes is the lucky character. The single word *Fook*, meaning luck, is painted on a diamond-shaped piece of red paper. Sometimes it is hung upside down. Then the word means "luck has arrived."

Arrangements of spring flowers are always shown at this time of year and they, too, have special significance. The plum blossom symbolizes longevity and courage. Another flower associated with the New Year is the water narcissus. Some Chinese believe if flowers blossom on New Year's Day, good fortune will be theirs for the next twelve months. Any flower or branch that blooms at this time of year is used in the decorations.

After the house has been prepared, it is time to bid farewell to the Kitchen God (*Tsun-Kwan*). In traditional China, the Kitchen God left the house on the twenty-third day of the last lunar month to report to the heavens on the behavior of the family. On this evening the family would give the Kitchen God a ritualistic dinner with sweet foods and honey. Today some families set up an altar offering sugarcane, honey, or oranges and offer a prayer that he will say "sweet things about them" after he leaves. It is customary to burn the Kitchen God's picture after the ceremony and to set off firecrackers outside the house to ward off evil spirits. It is believed the Kitchen God will return on the first day of the New Year.

After the Kitchen God has departed the house, final preparations begin. Families shop for new clothes to be able to start out fresh on New Year's Day.

Some people like to get their hair cut and washed. They believe this will bring them luck in the next twelve months.

Chinatown is bustling with activity now. The color red is seen everywhere, for in China the color red symbolizes happiness.

Everyone is shopping for special holiday foods and gifts.

*S*pecial New Year pastries are great favorites, particularly a traditional New Year's cake called *Nin Go*.

All the stores are decorated with spring couplets or scrolls. This one says "May everything be according to your wishes."

Storekeepers and creditors make a great effort to collect their bills. Everyone tries to pay his debts before the New Year.

This man is using an abacus. It is a centuries-old Asian calculator used by many Chinese-Americans today.

New Year's Eve is the most important time for the family. All generations gather together for the New Year's Eve feast. If someone is unable to be there, a place is set for him along with an empty chair to symbolize that person's presence. At the dinner, traditional holiday foods are served, such as fish, poultry, pork, beef, vegetables, and noodles. The poultry and fish are served whole to represent family unity.

Traditionally, New Year's Eve family dinners are held in the home, but today some Chinese-Americans gather their families together for a banquet in a restaurant. These spring banquets are held throughout the holiday.

In traditional families, the young members of the family bow and pay their respects to their parents and elders at midnight, following the banquet.

Children are allowed to stay up as late as they can on New Year's Eve. That night they usually receive red envelopes with good luck money (*Lai-See*) inside from their immediate family members. Only paper money is given since change is considered to be bad luck. Throughout the holiday, children will receive *Lai-See* from other married relatives and friends.

*S*ome people go to the temple on New Year's Eve to pray for their ancestors and for good fortune in the coming year.

On New Year's Day, everyone is on his best behavior. There are no bad words or bad manners. It is believed that whatever happens this day determines your luck for the year.

On this day, visiting begins. It is traditional to visit your grandparents and parents first, and then your friends. Throughout the holiday, friends gather to renew old friendships.

Guests usually bring a gift. It can be a potted, flowering plant or a New Year delicacy such as melon seeds, candied fruits, or New Year's cakes.

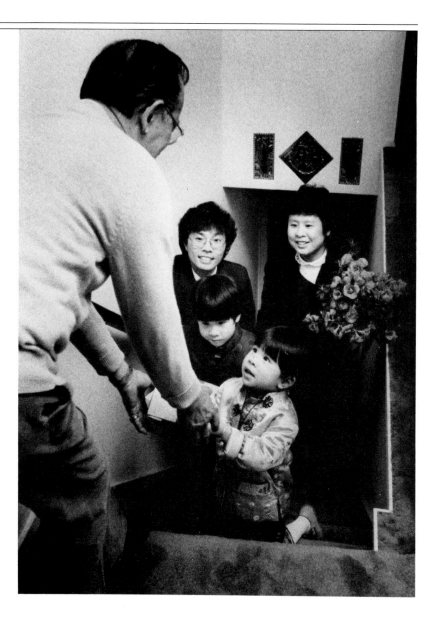

To welcome their visitors many families keep a tray of sweetmeats called a *Chuen-Hop*, or a "tray of togetherness." Traditionally, it has eight compartments, each with a special food item significant to the season. For example, it is thought that if you eat candied lotus seed, you will have sons. Eating candied melon promotes growth and good health. Candied coconut represents togetherness. Watermelon seeds symbolize "having plenty."

On the third to fifth days of the New Year, students from martial arts studios perform the lion dance in front of stores to scare away evil spirits and bring good wishes to the shopkeepers. The money given to them by the shopkeepers is donated to charity.

Everyone adds a year to his age on the seventh day of the New Year. In traditional China, individual birthdays were not considered as important as this New Year's date. Today the tradition is only symbolic of the festivity and happiness of the New Year.

The grand climax to the holiday is the dragon parade. For two centuries, the New Year festivities have ended on the fifteenth day of the first month with the celebration of the three-day lantern festival. Lanterns were carried through the streets. To complete the festivities, a paper, silk, and bamboo dragon went weaving through the streets amid strings of firecrackers. Today the lantern festival is no longer carried on in America, but the Chinatown parade continues the tradition of ending the holiday with a dancing dragon.

Today the Chinatown Golden Dragon Parade is a combination of old and new,

east and west,

with marching bands

and beauty queens.

At last, here comes the dragon!

Firecrackers explode everywhere, warding off evil spirits.

hat noise!

hat fun!

ung Hay Fat Choy!

About the Author

Tricia Brown is also the author of *Someone Special,
Just Like You*, and *Hello, Amigos!* A graduate student
in multicultural education, she lives near San
Francisco's Chinatown with her husband and seven-
year-old son. She has traveled extensively in Southeast
Asia and is a member of The Chinese Culture
Foundation.

About the Photographer

Fran Ortiz, an award-winning photojournalist for the
San Francisco Examiner, was also the photographer for
Someone Special, Just Like You and *Hello, Amigos!* In
1981 he was nominated for the Pulitzer Prize for his
social documentary on the Mono Indians. He lives in
Kensington, California, with his wife and young son.

SUN VALLEY SCHOOL
75 HAPPY LANE
SAN RAFAEL, CA 94901